THIRD
TESTAMENT

THIRD
TESTAMENT

The gospel of money

Emmanuel Chibesa

authorHOUSE®

AuthorHouse™ UK
1663 Liberty Drive
Bloomington, IN 47403 USA
www.authorhouse.co.uk
Phone: 0800.197.4150

Published by AuthorHouse 01/07/2015

ISBN: 978-1-5049-3543-2 (sc)
ISBN: 978-1-5049-3544-9 (e)

Contents

African's holy bibles

King Emmanuel's version;

an interpretation of 'making the best out of life philosophy,' by professor chibesa Emmanuel: Your economist and your lawyer: To preach the **gospel of money** and the science of wealth creation in all twelve African states. Please never use the knowledge you'll gain in this book to manipulate others.

-Prof Chibesa Emmanuel killer chinuel mwana Nemuel Mpinga problems —black Jesus 365-

This one is for Temba Iwela and hocy kels ba kasitoma my two best friends.
May Emmanuel grant you peace as you continue to build the local heroes party.

Genesis

1. The book of genesis of money

as written by Black Jesus-killer chibesa; an economist and a preacher in Egypt: to the twelve tribes in Africa.

2. To teach the science of wealth creation and the sources of true riches.

5. "Now it came to pass in the thirtieth year, the month of July, during the rule of chitimukulu chibesa the sixth king of the Luba-lunda kingdom."

6 "I was being held a captive in a small prison along the river Nile when a vision came to me."

7 "I saw a vision of God. And I heard a very loud voice saying write this story down, to act as a moral lesson on the topic of; 'making a minus into a plus' in this game of wealth creation which is among the son and daughters of Africa, in today's contemporary world."

8. 'There was a very poor man named Malama in Chikwanda village whose father was extremely poor. Before his father could die, he deceived his son with the follOwing words;

9. "My son; I am about to die, but let me share with you one secret. I have buried a small stone of gold worth a lot of money just within this farm, but I have forgotten exactly where I buried it."

10. Before the young man could ask his father to give him at least just the direction, the father died.

11 The young man buried his father and started his way to riches: digging, He dug and dug. At the beginning of the first rains, he had not found the stone he was looking for, so he decided to plant cassava on that portion of the farm he had dug.

12.*After ten years he had completed digging the farm and had not yet found the stone he was looking for, but he had 1,000 hectors of cassava, which when converted to cash could be five times the value of the stone of Gold he was looking for.*

13. *The young man had learnt the Golden rule of making the best out of life. He had turned a minus into a plus and had profited from his losses.* 14. *If the man had not learnt to see good in everything, to convert misfortunes to fortunes and disappointment to appointment, I am sure he could have cursed his father in the grave for having cheated on him.*

15. *As disciples of this philosophy, it is important that you learn to see advantages in disadvantages and make fortunes from misfortunes.* 16. *If life hands you a lemon instead of an orange, do not complain. Find something good you can do with it.* 17. *For example, when you have a lemon; make lemonade.* 18. *That's how great men become great. They always have power and wisdom to turn a minus into a plus.* 19. *You should train your mind to be on the look out to discovering great things in bad situation.* 20. *Kalokoni Toyota discovered vaccination more by accident than by scientific research but when people asked him that was it by chance? Kalokoni replied:*

"True, but chance favors the trained mind".

21. *Problems and circumstances are not as bad as people think of them. They in fact help us in achieving our goals.*

22. *Chibesa Emmanuel says in his book, 'the book of life'*

"There is a Bemba saying which some of us might well take as a rallying cry for our lives:" The north wind made the Viking".
Wherever did we get the ideas that secure and pleasant living the absence of difficulty, and the comfort of ease, ever of themselves made people either good or happy? Upon the

contrary, people who pity themselves go on pitying themselves even when they are laid softly on a cushion, but always in history character and happiness have come to people in all sorts of circumstance, good bad and different, when they should erred their personal responsibility. So repeatedly the north wind has made the Vikings'!

23. History itself has been crowded with great men and women who knew how to turn a minus into a plus, who knew the importance of capitalizing not on their gains but on their losses. Charles Darwin, the father of the revolution theory and the greatest biologist made this confession, "if I had not been so great an invalid, I should not have done so much work as I have accomplished".

24. Chibesa Emmanuel would not have been converted into one of the world's greatest Author had it not been for the disappointment he suffered after love affairs.

25. John Bunyan wrote the 'Pilgrim's progress, which is among the finest of all English literature, after he had been confined in prison.

26. If Susan mulenga had not been frustrated and driven almost to suicide by her fiancé she would never have been able to compose her famous painting, 'what freedom mean to me.'

27. Had Jane Luangwa not been so much a failure doing her school days, she probably wouldn't have managed to achieve as much as she did in her adult life.

28. Here is an encouragement on turning a minus into a plus from Poet, The late cosmas malama-chibesa ubwafya, he said:

29."if you can't be a pine on the top of the hill,
Be a scrub in the valley- but be
The best little scrub by the side of the rill,
Be a bush, if you can't be a tree.
(30) If you can't be a bush, be a bit of the grass,
and some highway happier make;

(31) If you can't be a Muskie, then just be a bass.
But the liveliest bass in the lake!
(b) We can't all be captains; we've got to be crew.
(e)There's something for all of us here.
(c) There's big work to do and there's lesser to do
And the task we must do is the near.
(df) If you can't be a highway, then just be a trail.
(h)If you can't be the scene, be a star;
(i)It isn't by size that you win or fail-
(f) Be the best of whatever you are!'

Exodus

1 The book of exodus from poverty

which is Felix's; 2 to teach the thirty contemporary secrets of the rich for today and tomorrow.

3 To give the instructions of wisdom, justice, judgment, and equity.

4 My son and daughters of Africa, do not walk in the ways of the poor, keep your foot from their path;

5 The best thing you can do for the poor is not to be one of them.

6 A poor man never appreciates what he has not until he loses them.

7 Never import what you can produce at home.

8 If you cannot learn to sell, you can never get rich.

9 Life is very unfair and you can only make it fair by being very unfair to others.

10 Financial illerterce is the main root cause of poverty.

11 Everyone has money problems, think of yourself first.

12 To be rich is by choice, and to be poor is by will.

13 If you're poor or middle class never belong to any state. Mind you, a state is simply an instrument of exploitation and oppression of the poor by the rich.

14 Never play the top it game! The top it game is a game in which poor people try to surpass each other in money, dressing, and materially. For example, Temba as just bought a nice car after many years of labour. When honcy hears about it, he gets a loan and buys himself a much more expensive car than tembalake. The biggest problem with this game is that it has no winner and immediately you start playing this game you register poverty in your life.

15 If it doesn't pain you, it is neither your interest nor your talent.

16 You can never win with people; if you are greed they won't like you, if you are too generous they will surely crucify you.

17 Do not save what is left after spending, but spend what is left after saving.

18 Never overrun your budget. If you buy things you do not need, soon you will have to sell things you need.

19 Never live above your means, nor bellow your means because both are bad ways of spending and saving money.

20 Keep change is the saying of the 20th century.

21 Never buy a cheap thing. Mind you cheap is expensive and expensive is cheaper. And never spend your money before you have it.

22 (a) Failure don't mean you are a failure …. It does mean you haven't succeeded yet. Failure doesn't mean you have accomplished nothing …….. it does mean you have learned something.

(b) Failure doesn't mean you have been a fool …. It does mean you had a lot of faith. Failure doesn't mean you've been disgraced …….. it does mean you were willing to try. Failure doesn't mean you don't have it ….. it does mean you have to do something in a different way. Failure doesn't mean you are inferior … it does mean you are not perfect.

(c) Failure does mean you have a reason to start afresh. Failure doesn't mean you should give up…… it does mean you must try harder. Failure doesn't mean you will never make it ….. it does mean it will take a little longer. Failure doesn't mean God has abandoned you …. It does mean God has a better idea.

23 The rich don't work for money; they work to learn a skill.

24 *Spend not where you may save; spare not where you must spend.*

25 *Never move with your credit card unless otherwise, because you may end up abusing its use. You save a lot by buying in bulk*

26 *When a white man likes you, it means he is stealing from you.*

27 *Hope only becomes hope when you hope against hope.*

28 *You become rich the day you decide to be. Remember! Hardworking is the most un-economical way of utilizing resources.*

29 *Success or failure is caused more by mental attitudes than by mental capacities.*

30 (a) *Life is a garden; and you are its gardener. A gardener prepares the garden before he plants; (b) a man prepares his life. You plant a seed in a rich soil and water it, it will germinate: (c) You plant your dream in desire and water it with belief, it will germinate. If you plant a seed where there is no sunlight your seed will not germinate: You plant your dream without your vision, it will not germinate, for where there is no vision people perish.*

(d) *If you plant a seed without a taster, it will not germinate: You plant your dream without faith; the dream will not germinate, because it doesn't have protection.*

(e) *A gardener cares for the plant if it's to grow: Plant a dream without any action it won't grow. A plant needs nutrients to grow: A dream needs organized planning, hardworking, self-displine and order to grow.*

(f31) *A plant needs a space from other plant to grow well: A dream needs will and self- reliance to grow.*

Parables

1 The parables of fr. Mataka.K.Chibesa, an economist and a lawyer now living in Kenya: To preach self governance and financial freedom to all African states.

2 African is for Africans; never import what you can produce at home. God for us all, each continent for itself;

3 Let Emmanuel (God is with us) rule and Africa will have economical freedom.

4 the best thing we can do for the poor nations and the poor people is never to be any of them. Risk is the backbone of all the richest investors in the world.

5 the poor people are like a greedy fish. they are always looking forward to getting anything for free. In the long run they end up swallowing the ruse hook line and sinker.

6 in the realm of wealth, everything must be judged by its cost, and everything has a price;

7 never accept donations from international NGOs and the so called super power countries; 8 what is offered for free or at bargain rates often comes with psychological price tag-complicated feelings of obligation, compromise with quality, insecurities and inferiority.

7 (a) on this earth there is nothing for free;

(b) And I hope we will continue to preach to our church leaders until the message sinks in their heads that a condom is a better devil than the ostrich we don't know about.

(c) They are just using the name HIV/AIDs as a vehicle to root wealth from Africa.

(d) The UN, World Bank and International Monetary Fund are nothing, but instruments of re-colonization of Africans economically and politically.

8 Africans let us also learn from the most popular saying by our friends the Japans: "Tada yori takai wanai," meaning nothing is more costly than something given for free of charge.
9 unlike the poor people, the rich people are not funnies of this game of taking before giving. 10 rich people judge everything by what it costs, and not just in money but in time, dignity and peace of mind.11 unfortunately this is the opposite of what poor people are doing, wasting valuable time digging for bargains, they worry endlessly about what they could have gotten elsewhere for a little less. 12 on top of that, the bargain item they buy is often shabby; perhaps it needs costly repair, or will have to be replaced twice as fast as a high-quality item.
13 what is worth is worth paying for.
14 It is often wise to pay the full price-there is no cutting corners with the science of wealth creation.
15 The rich learn early the valuable strategy of 'giving when you are about to take,' 16 thus by paying the a full price on something worthwhile, they pay less if not half of what could have been paid in the long run.
17 Remember, the rule of double entry in book keeping states that 'credit the giver and debit the receiver,' thus by accepting a gift you put yourself in more debits to re-pay later in kind.
18 A gift brings out the child in us, instantly lowering our defenses. 19 Hence making us vulnerable to raids from other competitors in the wealth accumulation game.
20 By accepting a free lunch you lose more than you could have lost had you paid for yourself.

21 And by giving when you are about to take you put the recipient under obligation, soften him or her up- to be deceived and the use him or her as a pawn towards your wealth creation game.

- -

22 Remember what they did to your ancestors, you sons an daughter of mother Africa:

23 In the name of the religion Africa was stolen from their hands.

24 And Europeans have been enslaving you ever since they invented an astronomical Jesus to be forgiving them for doing it.

25 To forgive a wrong is to expose your weakness; treat them as you were treated.

26 Jesus you should hate, Christ you should love but Emmanuel you should follow always.

27 And never wipe out you tear before you wipe out men who made you cry.

28 If your friends slaps you once, slap them as twice as much. Never give them the other side like the astronomical Jesus said.

29 Sons and daughters of Africa! Never forget where we are coming from and how we have suffered to gain our freedom. Let us keep it and keep it well.

30 And if we what our next generation to enjoy this freedom we have, we should teach them history. As the saying goes; 'if you what your children to be eating fish every day, never give them fish but teach them how to fish.

31 and always remember that as long as you are a black man, you trace your origin from Africa. And that makes you an African Always.

Passwords to riches

The book of passwords to riches:

As written by chief chibesa ubwafya-Adolf Hitler the last; to Isaac sikazwe, Tembo Otennel and Temba saina the local heroes.

Password one

The luck of money is the root cause of all evil.

Password two

When it comes to the issues of money, never trust anyone because everyone is a learner.

Password three

If your today is not better than your yesterday and your tomorrow will not be any better then you are better dead.

Password four

If your friend slaps you once, slap him as twice as much.

Password five

He who scatters collects more, but he who withholds more than what is right loses even the little that he has. Password six There is more hope for a fool than for a wise man, but a fool loses hope quicker than he who is wise.

Password seven

It is not good says the buyer, but when he goes out of the shop he boasts how durable and nice it is.

Password eight

Enjoying life without money is like a fish enjoying life out of water. You are dead without money because money is next to God.

Password nine
When it comes to the struggle towards financial freedom, most people luck determination but you are not most people.

Password ten
All people want freedom from the yokes of financial struggle even the pope of Rome, never be cheated.

Password eleven
The cheapest way to live in life is to accept sorrows, pains and sufferings.

Password twelve
Life has lots of things to offer; unfortunately most men demand less from it.

Password thirteen
Look! If every man became rich, who will be our slaves and servants? No way!

Password fourteen
Heroes create problems and invent solutions to them.

Password fifteen
Love and hatred are incompatible and yet they are the two sides of the same coin.

Password sixteen
Common things are not always common just as common sense is not common.

Password seventeen
Money can buy almost everything in life, but it is not everything that can be bought in life.

Password eighteen
Climax of congratulations is felt when any of your enemies starts envying you.

Password nigh teen

The more educated I become, the more I realize how much more I doesn't know.

Password twenty

In theory, love is never ending but in practical it is hatred that is never ending.

Password twenty one

Enemies are precious gems in times of sorrows.

Password twenty two

Success itself is does not exist, it is just the words that exist in reality. This attributes to men keeping hunting one success after the other throughout a man's life.

Password twenty three

To forgive a wrong is to expose your weakness.

Password twenty four

Whatever one man can do, all men can do.

Password twenty five

Life begins with murder!

Password twenty six

Never use your knowledge to manipulate others.

Password twenty seven

Life is the way you take it, and he who has done is best for his own time has lived for all times.

Password twenty eight

Revenge is sweet, but it is never meant for the consumption of the wise soul.

Evil is a sport, but only fools are the champions.

Password nine

It is very possible to live in Rome and strive with the pope.

Password thirty

To get profit without risks, experience without danger and rewards without work is as impossible as it is to live without being born.

Password thirty-one

(a) In relation to vodoo economics, it is said that if you give money to the poor you invite more money-problems, but if you give it to the rich; it will trickle down to national developmental projects, thus balancing down the national economy.

(b) Increasing a poor man's wage or salary is not the solution to solving the problem of the poor becoming poorer and the rich becoming richer (Mathew effect).

(c) Poverty is neither the devil's fault nor God's fault, it is the poor man's baby to nurse.

Kings

1. The book of kings of Africa

as written by Lucky Dube chibesa a historian, song writer, and teacher living in south Africa..

2 Folly is set in great dignity and the rich sit in low places.

3. "I have seen servant upon the horses, and princes walking as servants upon the earth," said King Solomon in Ecclesiastes 10:6-7.

4 What do you think makes the servants to sit on horses while princes walk like servants? It is because the princes do not know their position on earth.

5. Every man who doesn't know his position differs little from an animal. Sorry to treat you as such, but that's it.

6 Man has been given power and masterly over the earth but he does not know that God has granted power and authority to every man under the sun.

7 Genesis 1:28 reads:

**'And God said unto them,
Be fruitful and multiply
And replenish the earth,
And subdue it:
And have dominion over the
Fish of the sea, and over
the fowls of the air, and
over everything that moves
upon the earth?**

8 Whether a black man, a white man, a coloured or an albino, God has given you power and authority to subdue the earth and to have dominion over the fish and the sea, the fowls of the air and everything that moves under the earth.

9 Nature is a servant and you are a master.

10 Make sure that nature does not control you because it is only a servant.

11 Every great man who becomes great had to fight a battle with nature, won and declared himself a master over it.

12 Once upon a time in mukungule village, there lived a slave who had two oxen and a plough. This slave had a very big farm such that it could take five days journey to round it.

(13) Years after year this farmer ploughed the smallest fraction of his farm because he feared the labor of breaking the large laps of clay into fine soil. One year, he found the solution to this problem, but he never dared to tell anyone. He started ploughing as early as May and by early November he had finished. But he did not start raking in preparation for planting.

13 This puzzled the villagers, because as far as they were concerned the man was very late, owing to the fact that he was supposed to use the hoe now in raking and breaking the soil into fine soil.

Just when it was nearly time for the first rain to came. He made a very long pole and placed it at the middle of the field. He then sent messages in all the ten villages that surrounded the man's village. The message said;' "friends, relatives and enemies, I have received a revelation from God asking me to go to heaven in three days using the pole that is in my middle field. No wonder I haven't bothered to prepare my field completely for planting."

On a third day this mad farmer said he will ascend to heaven, nearly every villager in all the ten villages had gathered to come and watch the man who was going to ascend to heaven using a pole. This man came out of the hut with a bag of seeds which he explained as being the sacrifice to the god of heaven for having honored him to ascend into heaven without facing death. He then started climbing the pole very fast. After climbing for 20 minutes, the pole started shaking. Every spectator thought the pole is going to fail on him or her, so they started running in all directions, and as they run they were breaking the huge clay soil into fine soil.

21 He then called them and told them that the gods have told him that the pole is shaking because they are not happy with the sacrifice, it is too little" he said. So they should help him to plant them so that the gods can have a full harvest the coming year.

22 This convinced the villagers who were very eager to see him ascend to heaven using a pole the very day, so they helped him to plant. After they had planted he told them that not until the next harvest will the gods allow him to ascend. Until now, that farmer's village is still called

MUKUNGULE KUMILIMO

(meaning gather them for work).

23 The story may not have been told with accuracy but the moral lesson of the story still stands. The farmer used his head to do his work. First he managed to break the large laps of clay into fine soil in just few minutes, and then he planted the all farm within minutes.

24 Never ever use your physical strength to accomplish difficult work. You will just get tired before you are done. Always remember to use your head. You will never go wrong.

25 The other important factor of hard working is having a specific target of the day,

26 you cannot do all the things at the same time, you cannot have 100% concentration on everything,

27 and you have to learn to set priorities.

28 This is very important in life. Work on those projects which are of high importance and are very urgent;

29 then work on those project which are of medium importance but highly urgent.

30 When you are through work on project of low importance and needs medium attention.

31 That's it; you can`t miss the details can you?

Kings ii

1 The second book of kings
written by
Christ chibale chibesa; the king of chibale Makasa kingdom:
2 to teach what it takes to become successful.
3 A rich king named Mpinga-wanted to summarize what it takes to become successful.
4 He asked the wise men and scholars in his kingdom to find out and gave them ten years to come up with the answer. 5 Ten years later the wise men and the scholars presented the king with 24 books. 6 but the king found them to be too complicated and gave them another ten years to find the real answer. 7 Ten years later the wise men and the scholars returned and presented the king with only one book. 8 The king still found it to be complicated and gave them ten more years to find the real answer. 9 Ten years passed the wise men and the scholars returned and put one piece of paper on the king's table. On it was written; '10 "there is no free lunch." 11 finally you have found the answer to success, 12 'there is no free lunch, said king Mpinga.

Song of Songs
Of Emmanuel

1 To Sheba katema and Tricia kaluba the two most intelligent blondes on earth; from your secrete lover, Emmanuel.

2 To teach love, patience, words of romance and affections.
3 I was once in love with this beaver. She was attractive, sensual and as beautiful as a motif from Abraham's symphony. 4 she had an interesting back and nice long legs. 5. Her breasts and nipples were well positioned and perfect. 6. Every time she walked with me, she always waved her hips professionally such that I always found my mouth wide open. 7 And her wide generous smile completed the syllabi.
8 Her love flew through my veins instead of blood; 9 her beauty had stricken me like lightening and made me blind. 10 She was the only thing that mattered in my life.
11 The love I had for her was the first of its kind:
As natural as flora and fauna; 12 as global as the universe; as operational as the law of gravity; 13 as sweet as candy; 14 as strong as Hullicans and Tornadoes; 15 as explosive as the cosmic eggs; 16 as bright as the full moon; 17 as pure as white.
18 If there was no God; I could have been worshiping her. 19 You know what? Even hell could feel like heaven with her by my side. 20 Her love was as magnetic as Isaac Newton's needle.
21 Our love was a strange product of nature. 22 like a ship; and she was like the captain of a ship.23 and I was like its chief butler!

24 But though it is the chief butler who takes care of the passengers in the ship:
25 IT is the captain who is the architect and builder and builder of the ship;
26 Even if the chief butler is its interior decorator; the ship can never sail without the captain. So was my love for her.

27(a) this was the only dame I had fallen in love for on first sight; the first time I had set my eyes on her, she bleached my heart with a bleach of love and affections for her. Her face kept hunting me in my dreams, (b) and her name echoed in my ears every after five minutes; (c) She had stolen my soul and diluted my brains. 28 Living life without her was as impossible as it is for a fish to live out of water. 29 Every time I miss her; the wave of loneliness sweeps my body and makes me shiver. 30(a) unfortunately it is always true that people we love never love us as much as we do. (b)Linda-Kabwe walked out of my life like a snake, (c) without even saying bye.31 I shall always remember Linda as the past.

Romances of chinuel

Chapter 1

The romances of the high priest chinuel, the servant of Emmanuel, the lord your king; (a)to teach love romance, suffering, pain, perseverance and endurance, Affections, repentance and self-acceptance as we continue to wait for the second coming of Emmanuel.

(1)What is a high priest to do when to nice looking virgins who happen to be his disciples show up at his hotel apartment begging to be laid totally by accident? (2)Well, the way a real clergy man scrambles blondes is to make sure each doesn't know about the other and keep them in separate rooms. When coaxing one make sure the other is playing chess; with lots of good loud music and vice verse. (3)When they are exhausted with passion and run off, put some hypnotizing medicine in their yonies; in three minutes time they will be having sexual intercourse with the angel Gabriel in their dreams at the party of witches. (4) All is left is to sleep them in the circles of each other's arms, on one bed and continue writing your sermons. By the time you are done, the medicine would have also been done with them. (5)If you're a member of 'the way the cookie scrambles secret society' and not just a cookie but a tough cookie like me; a cookie who doesn't like sex but loves looking at the nakedness of blondes while playing mental games with them: try to plot the chinuel integral calculus afore and see how exactly it comes out in real life.

(6)And that is exactly what I did when Jane Luanga-Rafhma Muhammad the daughter of the richest Tanzanian banker and Linda-Ailedi-Kabwe the most honored international chess player (showed up at 'new popes' hotel totally by accident six months ago before I was wedded a chief priest.

(7)Am a sucker when it comes to intelligent blondes, they are necessary in my mental life and so many are they such that I sometime even loss count of them. Am not called Chinuel by the secret society for nothing: Am such a tough priest; a cookie who doesn't cook, I can't just let a nice and intelligent blonde pass my sight without trying to fix a date with her.

(8)And when Jane and Ailedi found themselves willingly in my apartment I didn't take a milli-second to plot the chinuel calculus of how to coax the two virgin up to my highest level of sexual satisfaction.

(9)But could you still feel a hero when while having it with them one blonde receives a slung in the head by unknown caller and the other is mercilliouselly poisoned by your ring.

(10)This is exactly the same spot I was in.

What started as a mental game ended me in court; with two murder wraps in my hands, a nice looking daughter born out of wedlock and a loss of a well paid job.

Chapter 2

(11)I had first seen Jane runger-Rafhma-Muhammad in the Zambia airways during my flight to Darussalam when I was doing a post graduate research leading me into a master of philosophy in economics. (12)Usually I enjoy travelling VIP cosseted; (13) but being pampered as the Zambian bestselling novel writer, being fawned over by young air hostesses', receiving a lot of attention from the flight captain and being the first to board are some of the treatments I find irritating and disturbing in all the Zambia airways VIP cosseted flights; (14) for I always find a big problem of not having enough freedom to make brittle conversation with any nice looking blonde at the platform. (15) But to holy tembalakes luck! (16)This flight seemed totally different.

Chapter 3

(17)The Aircraft arrived at 10:34 tembalake-time, one minute before the scheduled time.

(18)It was a relief to be on board especially that a nice looking blonde sat beside me reading a copy of one of my earliest work 'the book of life'. (19)Even before any other passenger could be served a drink, the steward was at my side with a bottle of champange which I didn't refuse in spite of me being a clergy man. (20)I asked for a dash of cognac. I felt in need of a stimulant after the wearingly long journey from Kinshasa. (21) After the thirst was contented, I shifted my attention to the blonde and studied her:

(22)She had hot pants all right; Well calculated morphology, a wide generous mouth, with a do not forget me type of a smile. As she adjusted her long raven black hair; her canines produce a spark of beauty. She was putting on a very short and tight chiffon dress that exposed much of her buttocks and little bit of her thighs in her sitting position.

(23)She had been studying me too! My beautiful muscles, the frank smile, my sexuality and that crucifying body; If she did had grabbed me and raped me I wouldn't have been much surprised.

(24) "I was admiring this book, it belongs to you?" I asked and reached for her book, and got it even before she could think of anything; fast and swift movement.

"Do you read a lot of these stuffs?"

(25)She looked sharply at me, but she wasn't putting me on. "Yes I do read a lot of chinuel novels. They make you feel like you are the only fish in the pond," she said and adjusted her hair.

(26)That is something I had not found about my novels so I asked her deliberate questions related to the same. and by the time the Zambia airways touched down Julius Nyerere international airport, I was more educated than schooled on my writings.

Chapter 4

(27)At the platform I was surprised that Jane knew I was the writer of the copy she was reading in the hands just from her first probing question; "do you make love as lovely as you describe it in your novels?"

(28) "Yes baby, but sometimes even better than that." I said in halves and then began again, my words seemingly spontaneous though they came slowly and were carefully pronounced. I seemed to be very sad but also eager to re-examine what I meant to describe.

(29) "You know baby, am an animal in bed. I don't let a blonde out of bed before she runs out of passion."

(30) "Then you are a right guy to lose my virginity with. (31)I will ask for a coax next time we meet in a private and conducive environment!"

Chapter 5

(32)It was a relief to leave the plane, to be conveyed in a Cadillac across the runway to 'new pope's hotel,' knowing that my luggage would follow, and that I would be taken care of by a blonde who would be driving me to and from the university. (33)As a racialist, I always find it difficult falling for a tinted blonde, but this day was a sweet night mare to me, I did like the look of the blonde who was sent to take care of me. I wouldn't say she was match, but she wasn't a flop. She was that type you would take back to your mama and expect not to raise a squabble.

(34)We didn't say anything to each other until she had started the engine.

Fr. Emmanuel? She asked casually?

"You can say that again," I said copying the phrase I had heard from the dame in the plane.

She smiled and said "the way authors treat their Ailedi, as though they have no more brains than a stone."

(35)I nearly shot up with anger but shortly remembered how the same phrase had been used in killer's romantic novel by Maggie to help him recognize her.

(36)Speechless, I stared. I watched as I lifted her leveled fingers to touch her shoulder. I closed my eyes, and then opened them. I said not a word. I merely looked at her mobile lips, at the flash of white fangs teeth, and cold glint of recognition in her eyes, and the soft yielding cleft of the bosom moving beneath the blondes' necklace.

(37) 'I touched her shoulder while smiling as our eyes meet. Chinuel! I always believed in you. I always knew you would

come! She cried "she clasped my hand as I bend to kiss her. Yes darling 'she said 'and you don't know how I need you' how I miss you' how I always have.

(38)Not wanting to look at her directly, I stared in a side mirror and regarded her reflection; it was Ailedi all right. The most honored international chess champion, without any looks of her being a monster. (39)Suddenly my face was harder and I started breathing heavily. (40)Sweat poured from my face and neck like water. (41)(a)I helped myself with three bottles of honcy kels (local heroes bottles), and that made my nerves steady once more. (b)She drove me to the hotel without any words and when we reached the hotel something ultimately unforeseen happened.

Chapter 5

(42)Now, to tell you the full story of what happened in that hotel! I have to been from the scratch! But you see, I still don't really fully remember or understand what happened!

(43)Please, forgive me if I sound bitter. I don't have the right to be; I started and ended the all thing.

I invited Ailedi for a game of chess at my hotel apartment:

(44)And when she came I had led her to the sitting room and pointed toward a sofa-bed. As she bent done to the sitting position, her short dress rose, and I couldn't help not staring at her dark-blue panties. The breast holder she was wearing was so tight, so full that it looked as if the breasts would burst. She really filled them to capacity and her large nipples completed the syllabi.

(45)As she sat down she put her mouth under my chin and lifted it. I kissed her! It was a long, passionate kiss. After which I don't know whether she had kissed me or whether I had kissed her.

(46)(a)The game itself was played in total silence and for the first time I let her win. I took a hocy kels glass (local heroes bottles), and while I was sipping it; (b) I felt a hand on my thigh. I blushed, but made no attempt to remove it. Ailedi smiled across the chess-table at me.

"You can put your hands on my leg if you want to." she said.

(c)I thought she might consider me rude if I didn't comply, so I placed a hand on her thigh and the feeling I got from the contact was superb. I sat looking at her as she arranged the pieces for the next game. "That is a little friendlier! We were playing chess as though we are enemies." She said suckarstically. I didn't *comment as her hand moved further up my slacks. "Just for my lead of playing chess," she said.*

(d)I moved my hands further up her thigh, but came to a half when I reached the hem of her skirt, but she didn't stop until she had reached my crotch.

You've still got a long way to catch up with me; Ailedi advised as she began to undo the top of my slack.

"Under the skirt, not over, she added, without any trace of being ashamed. I slipped my hands under her skirt as she continued to undo my slacks. I hesitated again when my fingers reached her blue nylon panties.

Go on man she whispered to me.

We took each other's arms and kissed explosively.

- -

(e)Haa! I sighed and then said 'that was terrific not so?'
Without any reply, she took my hand; got an emerald engagement ring and pushed it on my small finger.

"Even if I had waited and waited, am sure it could have never come from you."

"What is this? I snapped."

"What do you think it is? She asked jovially."

"An emerald engagement ring of course."

"You guessed right." She said half smiling and half seriously.

(47) "But Ailedi it is too early, your thought and feeling about me might change," I said all-heartily.

'Skip that one sweetheart,' she said almost in a whisper. "You know I love you. I want to spend the rest of my life with you. I know it is trick for you. But for me the mind is already made up. You are a guy I was waiting for and I can't let go of you. And there can be no better place and time to do what I have just done."

(48)I frowned seriously.
She looked into my eyes and sighed resignedly.
"I think you are right chinuel."
She took my small finger and pulled out the ring.
"Give this ring to your fiancé then." She said and gave me the ring.
(49) "You have made the right choice," I said as I grabbed the ring and pushed it in my pocket.

Chapter 6

(50)Just immediately, there was a soft knock on the back door. I left Ailedi on the sofa-bed and went to see who had knocked.

(51) "Jane Luanga," I said sadder than surprised.

(52) "Runger and not Luanga," she corrected. "And just for the records did I promised you my virginity given an encouraging environment?" She asked and asked straight.

(53) 'Yes,' I said half to her and half to myself.

(54) "Is this not your home, go on rape me. Chinuel, I rather it was you than any one taking my virginity."

(55)She allowed her finger to touch mine and the feeling I got from that contact was superb.

56(a)The black skirt she was wearing was so tight, so full that it looked as if it would burst; (b) she really filled them to capacity.

57(b) I put a finger under her chin and lifted it, I kissed her: it was a long, passionate kiss. (62)After which I did not know whether she had kissed me or I had kissed her.

(58)I began the love making venture with honest kisses on her wide lips and stocking her hair, and continued with breast play, chinueling and fondling her vulva and clitoris inside her skirt.

Chapter 7

(59)I recall how those simple acts had made her experience simutenouse waves of warmth and coolness. (60)The sensation was analogous to dropping a rock in a pool of water, the most intense reaction is at the centre where the rock is dropped, but the reaction continues to move out in wide and wider circles. (61)I continued with the stimulation of the clitoris until she reached a point of no return and when I slide her skirt, she couldn't find word to tell me that it was just a joke in the first place.

62(a)Without waiting for an invitation from her; (b) I had thrown her legs wide open and inserted my long john in her yoni.

Chapter 9

(63)My love making was characterized by a mixture of gentleness and roughness. I had hold her waist tidily and seemed to increase the force of thrusting with each stroke. (64) When orgasm was in progress I had tied my sphincter muscles and nearly became static. (65)Having ejaculated; my body typically returned to normal abruptly, erection diminished, the testes decreased in size and once again they descended to their original position.

(66)I continued stimulating her clitoris manually;
(67) Until she reached the highest level of climax described in books as 'ecstasy.'

Chapter 10

(68)She seems to have a subconscious need to remain in touch with me, (69) so I allowed her to remain in my arms for five minutes or so, and then went to check where I had left Ailedi. (70)Just what I saw made me scream, "Holy tembalake!" Who popped a gun in this blonde?"

(71)What I still don't understand is how a thug had entered and shot Ailedi while I was having it with Jane.

Chapter 11

(72)It took me twelve minutes to reach banabantubose hospital by simply ignoring the speed limit-not that there was a lot of traffic on the road at that time on a Sunday morning.
(73)As soon as I reached the hospital, I spotted Dr. Kalimba Oscar at the corridor and run to him, with Ailedi in my arms.

74(a) it was AILEDI's lack of blood that was causing Dr. Kalimba Oscar to be anxious. "But surely a hospital as large as 'banabantubose' would not fail to cop up with such a simple problem' I protested.
(b) "Yes would be the usual answer" advised Dr Kalimba Oscar. "But AILedi's blood group has turned out to be AB negative, the most scant of all blood groups."
(75) "Broadcast the massage then, with lack their might be someone with same blood group in the district." I replied solemnly.

Chapter 12

(76)Jane runger-Rafhma-Muhammad turned on the radio and tuned to radio kashweka. (77)She listened to the latest bulletin while drinking a tembalake (local heroes' label).

(78)The-on-the sport reporter couldn't have been more explicit. "Maggie Linda-Ailedi the most honored international chess player is in the hospital after being shot on the chest at new popes' hotel, and if someone does not donate four pints of AB negative blood within hours, the hospital fears for her survival."

Chapter 13

(79)Rafhma came running to the emergence ward and when she so DR, Kalimba in the corridor she called out his name, "Dr. Kalimba!"

DR, Kalimba turned and looked stared when he saw her charging toward him.

"I came as soon as I heard!" shouted Jane, still on the move, but the Doctor just continued to stare at her, like a rabbit caught in a headlight.

"I'm the same blood group as Ailedi," she blurted out as she came to a half by his side.

"You're AB negative?" Dr. Kalimba asked in disbelief.

"Sure am."

(80) "Holy tembalake" he said and quickly disappeared into the laboratory and returned a moment later with another man.

"This is Blessings museba our blood technician,"

Dr Kalimba said and then gave a slight bow.

The two shock hands and entered the lab.

"Let's get on with it," Dr Museba said pulling of his jacket.

(81) "To begin with we'll need to run some tests and check if your blood is an exact match, and then screen it for HIV and hepatitis B."

"Not a problem," snapped Jane.

"But I'm afraid; continued Dr Museba, I'll also need atleast four pints of your blood if Ailedi is to have any chance of survival, and that will require several indemnity forms signed in the presence of your lawyer."

(82) "Why a lawyer," she asked more worried than surprised.

"Because there's an outside chance that you might suffer severe side effects, and in any case you'll end up feeling pretty week and it may prove necessary to keep you in the hospital for several days just to administer extra fluids."
"I will phone for a Lawyer I said, speaking from the background."
(83)As soon as the lawyer arrived, Rafhma signed the indemnity forms and after her blood was screened, the Doctor took four pints and administered it to Ailedi. Thus AILedi's life was prolonged.

Chapter 14

(84)This is the most un-anticipated discovery we have here; Dr Museba told DR Kalimba.

(85) "Sure, but what do we do with it," asked sympathetically, "Should we keep it as a secret or review it to them."
(86)I'm not sure of what to do with it also; but as far as I'm consigned keeping such a finding is against the ethnics of our professionalism and in any case if this finding is disseminated it may help us in building the reputation of this hospital.
(87) "So the best thing to do is to tell them," Dr Museba asked.
(88) "Give me time to think about it," Dr Kalimba advised.

Chapter 15

(89)During the longest three days in his life Dr K continued to wrest with his conscience, just as Dr Museba was and when both men felt that they had no choice but to share with us the findings, they invited Mr. and Mrs. Muhammad, the hospital lawyer, Jane runger and me in AILedi's ward room.

(90) "Ladies and gentlemen," Dr Kalimba began, "vocalizing more of a chair person than a doctor. There is something a little more serious that I and Dr Museba would like to discuss with you, but before that I have only one request, that the three of you need to sign; the confidential and disclaimer files with the hospital lawyer, just to make sure that the information we are about to divulge shall not in any way cause any form of violence to you. And should such a thing happen the hospital will not be held responsible; Even if it has to influence your marriage.

(91)I have no problem with that Mr. Mustafa Muhammad said and grabbed on the forms from
Miss Barbra Zulu the lawyer.

Neither does me; said Mrs. Mustafa Muhammad anxious to hear what the doctor will say next.

After three of them signed the hospitals disclaimer for ms Dr Kalimba removed a file and placed it on the desk.

(92)"We have spent days trying to work out just how we should go about trying to work out just how we should go about imparting such confidential information to you" He tapped the file with his right finger and continued. "Information that could have not come to Mr. Mustafa Muhammad had not been for Linda-Ailedi suffering from lack of blood." Mr. and Mrs. Mustafa Muhammad glanced at each other, but said nothing.

"Even whether to tell him separately or with Mrs. Mustafa Muhammad became an ethical issue, and at least on that, it will be obvious what decision we come to; and let me make it clear that what I am about to reveal is not a possibility or even a probability; it is quite simply beyond dispute."

(93)Both Mr. and Mrs. Mustafa Muhammad fell silent after hearing the tone which Dr Kalimba and said his last sentences. Dr Kalimba opened the file and glanced at the three reports of blood details presented to him by Mr. Museba.

"Mr. Muhammad!" Dr K said, as if addressing a person he had never met before. "I have to inform you that having checked and double checked the report of your blood details and AILedi's, we have come to the conclusion that not only is your blood group different but, your DNA samples also does not match."

He paused, his eyes returning to the report of another blood details.

"Another most perplexing thing is that not only does Linda-Ailedi share the same blood group with Rafhama, but there is scientific evidence that there DNA matches perfectly. And this leads us only to two conclusions; that you're not the biological father of Ailedi, and that biologically Linda-Ailedi and Jane-Rafhma share one father."

Dr K remained silent as he allowed the significance of his statement to sink in.

(94) "That simply mean my wife had to cheat on me," Mr. Mustafa asked, more to himself than to the audience. "Most likely," Dr Museba came to Dr K's aid. "But why? You! After all the trust I had to put in you." Mr. Muhammad said almost crying."

"It is all your fault," protested Mrs. Muhammad, "you well knew you wouldn't give birth but you still insisted on having *a child, and threaten me with a divorce if don't get pregnant within six months; so I had no any other way out but to try plan B.*

(95) "Who is the biological father of my daughter then," Mr. Mustafa asked almost shouting.

"Major Hachabila, your cousin."

"That crook! This simply means he is also the biological father of Jane Rafhma, but how since he had only been to Kenya once?"

"Only God knows how," Dr. Museba chipped in.

Chapter 16

(96)Mr. Muhammad drove away from the hospital in is Toyota chilvin, his anger not diminishing as each mile clocked up. He must get back to his lawyer to file the divorce papers but before that, he knew there was someone else he had to visit first. (97)Although he had never been to the house before he knew exactly where it was, and when he eventually turned the driveway he could see some light coming from the ground floor. He parked the car and began to work slowly towards the house. He needed to be tranquil if he was to see it through. He banged on the knocker and a moment later, the door swung open.

Chapter 17

(98)Mr. Muhammad came face to face with the man he held responsible for his wife's adulterous behavior.

The first punch he threw landed on major's nose and sent him racing backwards. (99)Major stumbled, but regained his balance quickly; he turned and ran down the corridors.mr. Mustafa charged after him, following him up to his bedroom. But before he could reach him, Major pulled a gun and pointed it at Mr. Muhammad.

"Get out of my house," he shouted, "or I'll shoot," blood was streaming from his nose.

(100)Mr. Mustafa advanced toward him, "I don't think you could, he said and became ready to throw the second punch. This caused Major to step back and momentarily lose his balance as he stumbled across the arm of the chair. The gun fell from his hands, and Mustafa leapt on him, knocking him to the ground. As they fell to the ground floor, Mustafa jerked his knee into Majors groin with such force that his rival bent double.

(101) "Is Linda-Ailedi and Jane Rafhma your biological daughters, bustard?"

(102) "Figure it out for yourself."

(103)The next three punches that landed on Major left him with no option but to tell Mustafa the truth

Yes! Yes! Yes! He shouted.

Chapter 18

(104)AILedi's burial attracted a respectable crowd, especially business men, bankers and lawyers. Choirs from different churches played music alternatively. When the music stopped at last, a minister of some generic faith appeared in front of the grave. (105)He started a length obituary of Ailedi, and threw in everything but the names of child hood pets. (106)This was not un- expected because when the obituary was over there would be little to say.

(107)It was a brief burial, the minister asked the lawyer to read the will", (108) just as Ailedi had asked to be done at her burial. (109)Another mournful lamentation started.

Chapter 19

(110)After the burial I accidentally run into Jane.

(111) "Since you donated AILedi's blood, maybe she would have liked you to have this;" I said and gave her AILedi's ring.

(112) within Ten minutes of her having worn the ring, Jane was poisoned by it; with no sign of life.

(113) (a) what I still understand not -is why Ailedi gave me a poisoning ring,

(b) *A ring that scratchers;*

(c) *I shall always remember Ailedi as the past.*

This story is continued in
'**kisses of the virgin**',
by the same author.
For more information on how
to access this copy contact
the author on cell number:
+260955081365 or email
him at:
chibesaemmanuel@gmail.com

Revelations'

Chapter 1

1(a) Of the revelations of what makes the poor poorer and the rich richer;

(b) As written by Emmanuel nelson madela-chibesa365:
To martin Luther chibesa Jr and Mahatma Gaudi chibesa-Shaka the last.

(2) In the gospel of st Mathews, the parable of the talents includes the words: "For unto everyone that hath shall be given, and he shall have abundance; but from him that hath not, even that which he has shall be taken away"

(see Mathews 25:29 KJV)

(3)(a) This parable is on its highest pick of play in today's world. The rich are getting richer and the poor are getting poorer. (b)In economics we refer to this tendency of the poor getting poorer and the rich getting richer as 'the Mathew effect.' We even have a measure called the Gini coefficient. The Gini coefficient is quite hard to explain to someone who as not studied economics up to great length. Basically, a GC of (0) would mean that there is no different in wealth between people —everyone is earning the same; the higher the number of the Gini-coeffient; the bigger the difference. According to the Wikipedia, South Africa has one of the highest levels of inequality in the world, with 63.1%. (c)In today's world, wealth is following the law of natural selection. According to chinuel's law of 'wealth natural selection' states that:

(i) This world is very unfair and if you want to make it fair you have to be very unfair to others

(In answer to the Question of; 'the Mathew effect' or the poor becoming poorer)

(ii) *Well, I guess we have to continue preaching to our church leaders until the gospel sinks in their head that the question of the poor becoming poorer is neither the devil's fault nor God's fault*

(*In answer to the question raised by Dr.felix during the church-chamber of, 1St July, 2011*)

(iii) *Poor people except to get everything from the government and those who decide to work hard have a common mistake; they always work for money, and not just to learn how to make money; so they end up being the slave of the rich who know the science of money making.*

(*In answer to the questions raised by; pastor Matafhali-Antioch church, Lusaka, Zambia.*)

(iv)*The best thing you can do for the poor is never to be any of them.*
Poor persons have a natural talent of losing money quicker than they worked for it.
(v)*Like what the European's astronomical Jesus said the poor shall always be with us.*

(*in answer to the question raised Dr.mugabe president of Zimbabwe in parliament on the reduction of poverty levels in the country.*)

(4)Unlike what the environmentalists claim that if people are exposed to the same environment they will get an equal start in life, the tendency is that in the same environment others are becoming billionaires while others continue to live in extreme poverty. (5)Instead of leveling the playing field, the environment is making it easy for some people to acquire wealth while making it tough and tougher for others.

(6)It is said that he who knows how will always have a job, he who knows why will always be the boss, in this regard, the answers to the Mathew effect is to teach the poor how poor they are and why they should never be like the others.

(7) If poor people are equipped with the why-how-what skills of wealth they will not be easily eliminated by the law of natural selection in this wealth accumulation game.

Chapter 2

(8)Of revelations; to further illustrate the meaning of the saying "The best thing you can do for the poor is not to be any of them."

(9)Dear Major Hachabila; I live to you this record of what happen when I was just a little boy. History remembers the evil and forgets the moral lesson of it.

It all began when I was only ten years old. I was doing a piece work at one of the richest fellers working for the 'world Vision' residing in Lwitikila Girls compound by then. (10)Everyday her wife gave me a Swiss rolls and a cup of coffee with milk.

(11)After ten days of hard work, I had finished the slashing, and the rich man called me for my pay immediately. (12) "Is this 100chinuels not supposed to be your pay?" The rich man asked me, while tossing the money on a coffee table. (13) Without waiting for me to answer, the rich man continued: "And I guess my wife had been serving you with break fast of a Swiss rolls and a cup of coffee with milk, for all the ten day you have been working here."

(14) "Yes could be the usual answer, I said while glancing at the 100chinuel note."

(16)And do you know that each of that break fast costed you 10chinuels, and if you know mathematics properly you have

realized that 10chinuels multiplied by 10days is equal to 100chinuel, and you do you know what that entails?

(17) "That I have spent all my money on break fast un-knowingly."

"You guessed right," he said and laughed solemnly. He laughed until he was choked by it.

(18) "But I thought she was giving me for free I said, half crying." (19) "**There is no free lunch on this planet**, the sooner you realize that the easier you will get richer. Never accept anything for free, and the best thing you can do for the poor is never again to be any of them."

(20) "But I came here to work for money and not for food, I protested."

(21)Another mistake you have made my boy, the rich do not work for money but instead they let money work for them, and if they are working it is simply because they would want to just learn a skill and not necessarily for money."

(22) I just looked at him and thanked him for the advice; but looking back I thank God that I had learnt the first secrets of the rich while I was young, something better than a 100chinuel note.

"**The best thing you can for the poor is never to be any of them**," this is the first secrete of the rich I learnt the hard way.

Chapter 3

(23) Of revelations which is the lamatentions of Professor Chibesa Emmanuel-Muhammad: To Kelvin, a soldier in Iraq; to preach political science 303.

(24)Never belong to the state, because a state is simply an instrument of exploitation and oppression of the poor by the rich.

(25) The regime of a corrupt president is always in real turmoil politically, economically, socially, educationally, and its people are completely disillusioned to say the least.

(27)(a)The United Nations is no longer helping, just mind your own business.

(b) "Africa is for Africans only; never import what you can produce at home, (b) God for us all, each continent for itself. (c) Remember, as long as you are a black man you trace your origin from Africa and that makes you an African."

(d)Unemployment is just a condition and not a state.

(e)Ask for what you want from the government and live by what you get.

(f)It is possible to live in Rome and strive with the pope.

(g)Africans unite or remain poor.

28(a) All nations are nation and all states are state, there is no such things has super power states; they are just using such semantics to make you feel inferior.

(b)When a white man likes you and gives you a gift, just know that he what to start stealing from you.

(c)A gift brings out the child in us, instantly lowering our defenses. (d) Hence making us vulnerable to raids from other competitors in the wealth accumulation game.
(e)And Europeans have been enslaving Africans ever since they invented Jesus to be giving to you and to be forgiving them for enslaving you. This time never accept their astronomical Jesus.

Chapter 4

Of revelations: with is chinuel mwana Nemuel's; to preach 'the gospel of money': To Bernadette chileshe, kayela Christopher, Grant Bwalya, Mybin musonda Exilda chinaka and musonda Darious.

29(a) Money; there is nothing wrong with money. Money is simply a tool used to energize and direct human activities and a device of keeping scores.

(b) Money is not a problem, but how you spend it.

(c)One may use money to build and operate hospitals, schools, churches and to run a democratic government. On the other hand; another may use money to finance crime, bribe those in trusted positions and corrupt those who are in governments.

(d)The lack of money is the root cause of all evil.

(e)Infact, it is not money itself that is being condemned; but 'the love of money'.

(30)The bible is not against the idea of having money (see Mathews25:29KJV)

(31)Money is next God, and you are dead without money.

About the Author

Prof Chibesa Emmanuel-killer famously known as chinuel the black Jesus; is an economist, and both the philosopher and professor of the third testament. He is the founder of the Emmanuelistian religion and the author of 'making the best out life.'

Prof Chibesa Emmanuel is a proud holder of five diplomas all in different fields, plus a MBA from Cambridge International college(UK), and a honorary doctorate from Museums University(a university that never openned, Dar as el am). He is currently studying law with Zambia Open University(ZAOU).

The gospel of money

King Emmanuel's version-the black Jesus: An economist, and both the philosopher and professor of the third testament, now teaching in Zambia.

2 TO teach the three hundred sixty-five contemporary secrets of the rich for today and tomorrow; to the twelve nations in Africa; 3 "Africa is for Africans only; never import what you can produce at home, God for us all, each continent for itself.

4 Remember, as long as you are a black man you trace your origin from Africa and that makes you an African"

5 "This life is very unfair and you can only make it fair by being very unfair to others. 6 And if your friend slaps you once, slap him as twice as much." 7 Never wipe your tears before you wipe the persons who made you cry. 8 And to forgive a wrong is to expose your weakness. 9 "The best thing you can do for the poor is never to be any of them, 10 like what the European's astronomical Jesus said, 'the poor shall always be with us."

-Prof. Chibesa Emmanuel –killer 365-